K. CONNORS

Youtube Starter Kit

The Ultimate Guide to Creating, Growing, and Monetizing Your Channel for Success

Copyright © 2024 by K. Connors

All rights reserved. No part of this publication may be reproduced, stored or transmitted in any form or by any means, electronic, mechanical, photocopying, recording, scanning, or otherwise without written permission from the publisher. It is illegal to copy this book, post it to a website, or distribute it by any other means without permission.

First edition

This book was professionally typeset on Reedsy.
Find out more at reedsy.com

Contents

Introduction: Welcome to Your YouTube Journey	1
Chapter 1: Finding Your Niche	6
Chapter 2: Planning Your Channel	10
Chapter 3: Setting Up Your Channel	16
Chapter 4: Creating High-Quality Content	23
Chapter 5: Optimizing for Search and Discovery	30
Chapter 6: Growing Your Audience	37
Chapter 7: Monetization Strategies	43
Chapter 8: Legal and Ethical Considerations	50
Chapter 9: Building a Personal Brand	56
Chapter 10: Long-Term Growth and Sustainability	62
Conclusion: Your YouTube Journey Awaits	69

Introduction: Welcome to Your YouTube Journey

Hey there, future YouTube star! If you're holding this book, you're probably itching to dive headfirst into the world of video creation, vlogging, and maybe even becoming the next big internet sensation. Well, you've come to the right place. The "YouTube Starter Kit" is your all-in-one guide to kickstarting your YouTube channel, growing an audience, and, yes, even making some money along the way.

The Purpose of This Book

Let's get one thing straight: this book isn't some dry, boring manual. Think of it more like your trusty sidekick on your YouTube adventure. Whether you're here because you want to share your passion for knitting tiny hats for cats, or you're convinced your daily life is entertaining enough to attract millions, we've got you covered. We'll walk you through everything from figuring out what you should make videos about to understanding the mysterious YouTube algorithm. By the end of this book, you'll have the confidence and knowledge to hit that record button and share your unique voice with the world.

The Importance of YouTube Today

YouTube isn't just a platform; it's a cultural phenomenon. It's the second most visited website in the world, just behind Google, its parent company. With over 2 billion logged-in monthly users, it's safe to say YouTube is where the action is. It's where people go to learn how to fix a leaky faucet, get the latest news, or laugh at cats doing hilariously dumb things.

And let's not forget the monetary aspect. You've probably heard stories of YouTubers making a living—sometimes even a fortune—by creating content. Sure, it takes time and effort, but it's totally doable. This book will help you understand the pathways to monetize your content, from ad revenue to sponsorships and beyond.

Who This Book is For

You might be wondering, "Is this book right for me?" Well, if you have an internet connection and a desire to create, the answer is a resounding yes. This book is for:

- Aspiring YouTubers who are just starting out and need a roadmap.
   - Hobbyists who want to share their passions with the world.
   - Marketers looking to leverage YouTube for their business.
   - Anyone who's ever thought, "Hey, I could do that!" while watching their favorite YouTuber.

Whether you're young or old, tech-savvy or a total newbie, there's something in this book for you. We'll keep things simple and straightforward, with a sprinkle of humor to keep it fun.

How to Use This Book

Think of this book as your personal trainer, but for YouTube. You don't need to read it cover to cover (though you totally can if you want to). Feel free to jump to the sections that interest you the most. Stuck on what kind of content to create? Head to the chapter on finding your niche. Need tips on editing?

INTRODUCTION: WELCOME TO YOUR YOUTUBE JOURNEY

There's a whole section on that too.

Here's a pro tip: don't just read—do. After all, the best way to learn is by doing. So, when we suggest brainstorming video ideas, grab a notebook and start jotting them down. When we talk about setting up your channel, follow along on your computer. This book is designed to be interactive and actionable.

Setting Expectations

Before we dive into the nitty-gritty, let's talk about expectations. Building a successful YouTube channel takes time, effort, and a bit of patience. You might not go viral overnight, and that's okay. The key is consistency and learning from each video you create. Celebrate small milestones, like your first subscriber or your first hundred views. These little victories add up and keep you motivated.

Real-Life Success Stories

To get you inspired, let's look at a couple of real-life success stories. Take the case of Jenna Marbles. She started her YouTube channel back in 2010 with a funny video about how to trick people into thinking you're good looking. That video went viral, and she's now one of the most recognized faces on YouTube. Or consider Marques Brownlee (MKBHD), who started making tech review videos as a teenager. Today, he's one of the most respected tech reviewers, interviewing the likes of Elon Musk and Bill Gates.

These YouTubers didn't start with fancy equipment or professional editing skills. They started with a passion and a willingness to put themselves out there. And guess what? You can too.

Your First Steps

Alright, enough with the pep talk. Let's get down to business. Your first step is to decide what you want your channel to be about. Don't worry if you're not 100 percent sure right now. This book will help you refine your ideas and find your unique angle. Think about your interests, your skills, and what you enjoy watching on YouTube. Chances are, there's an audience out there for whatever you're passionate about.

Once you have a rough idea, it's time to plan. Yes, even the most spontaneous-looking videos usually have some level of planning behind them. We'll guide you through creating a content plan that keeps you organized and helps you stay consistent with your uploads.

And of course, there's the technical stuff. Setting up your channel might seem daunting, but it's really not. We'll walk you through the process step-by-step, from creating your YouTube account to optimizing your channel layout for maximum appeal.

A Few Words on Motivation

Creating content regularly can be challenging, especially when you're just starting out and the views aren't rolling in yet. Here's the thing: every successful YouTuber started with zero subscribers. The difference between those who succeed and those who don't is perseverance. Keep creating, keep learning, and don't get discouraged by slow growth. Remember, it's a marathon, not a sprint.

Stay Connected

One of the coolest things about YouTube is the community. Don't be afraid to engage with other creators, join forums, and participate in social media groups. You'll find support, collaboration opportunities, and a lot of great advice from people who've been where you are.

Final Thoughts

INTRODUCTION: WELCOME TO YOUR YOUTUBE JOURNEY

So, are you ready to start your YouTube journey? With this book in hand, you have all the tools and knowledge you need to go from newbie to pro. We'll be with you every step of the way, offering tips, tricks, and a little bit of humor to keep things light. Remember, the most important thing is to have fun and let your personality shine through. After all, that's what makes YouTube so special—it's a platform where you can be yourself and connect with people from all over the world.

Now, let's get started! Your audience is out there, waiting to discover your amazing content. Lights, camera, action!

Chapter 1: Finding Your Niche

Alright, let's dive into one of the most crucial steps in your YouTube journey: finding your niche. Think of your niche as your channel's identity, its unique flavor that makes it stand out in the vast sea of content on YouTube. This chapter is all about helping you discover what makes you special and how to carve out a space for yourself in the YouTube universe. Ready? Let's go!

Identifying Your Passion and Interests

First things first, let's talk about passion. No, this isn't a pep talk from your high school career counselor. It's practical advice. Creating content takes time and effort, so you'll want to focus on something you genuinely enjoy. Ask yourself: What are you passionate about? What topics can you talk about for hours without getting bored?

Here's a little exercise to get you started. Grab a notebook or open a notes app on your phone. Make a list of things you love doing, hobbies you're obsessed with, or subjects you're always curious about. Don't hold back. This is your brainstorming session, and there are no wrong answers. Do you love cooking exotic dishes? Are you a fitness enthusiast? Maybe you're a tech geek who's always tinkering with the latest gadgets. Write it all down.

Now, look at your list and pick a few topics that really jump out at you. These are the things you could see yourself creating videos about consistently.

Remember, passion is key. If you love what you're doing, it will show in your videos, and your audience will pick up on that enthusiasm.

Researching Popular Niches

Once you've identified your passions, it's time to do a little market research. Don't worry, you won't need a business degree for this. The goal here is to find out if there's an audience for the topics you're interested in. After all, you don't want to pour your heart into a series of videos that no one watches.

Start by doing a simple YouTube search for your topics. See what kind of content already exists. Pay attention to the number of views, the subscriber counts of the channels, and the level of engagement in the comments. This will give you an idea of how popular your chosen topics are.

Next, check out Google Trends. This handy tool lets you see how often particular topics are searched for on the internet. Enter your topics and compare their popularity over time. Are they trending upwards or downwards? This can help you gauge the long-term potential of your niche.

Don't be discouraged if you see a lot of content already out there. That's actually a good sign! It means there's an audience for it. The trick is to find your unique angle.

Evaluating Your Unique Angle

Alright, you've identified your passions and done some research. Now it's time to figure out what makes you different. This is your unique selling point, or USP. It's what will make viewers choose your channel over someone else's.

Think about your personality, your skills, and your experiences. How can you bring something fresh to your chosen niche? Maybe you have a quirky sense of humor, or you're an expert in a specific subfield. Perhaps you can combine two interests to create a unique blend. For example, if you love fitness and cooking, why not create a channel focused on healthy recipes and workout tips?

Here's another exercise for you. Write down a few sentences that describe what makes you unique. Try to be as specific as possible. Instead of saying, "I'm funny," say, "I have a dry, sarcastic sense of humor that I use to make people laugh while educating them about personal finance." See the difference?

Case Studies

To give you a little inspiration, let's look at some real-life examples of successful niche channels.

Meet Sarah, the creator behind the channel "Budget Girl." Sarah's passion is personal finance, specifically helping people get out of debt and live frugally. What makes her unique? Her down-to-earth, relatable approach. She shares her own financial journey, complete with mistakes and successes, and offers practical tips that anyone can follow. Sarah's authenticity and willingness to share her personal story have earned her a loyal following.

Then there's "Brandon the Tech Guy." Brandon loves technology, but so do a million other YouTubers. What sets him apart is his focus on affordable tech for everyday people. While other tech channels review the latest high-end gadgets, Brandon reviews budget-friendly options and shows viewers how to get the most bang for their buck. His practical, no-nonsense approach has made him a go-to resource for viewers looking to save money without sacrificing quality.

Your unique angle doesn't have to be groundbreaking. It just needs to be true to who you are and resonate with your audience.

Takeaways

Alright, let's recap the key points and actionable steps to help you find your niche:

Identify Your Passions: Make a list of things you love and are passionate about. Focus on topics that you can talk about endlessly.

Research Popular Niches: Use YouTube and Google Trends to see how popular your chosen topics are. Look for high engagement and upward trends.

Evaluate Your Unique Angle: Think about what makes you different. What unique perspective or skills can you bring to your niche? Write down a few sentences that capture your uniqueness.

Study Successful Channels: Look at successful YouTubers in your niche and see what makes them stand out. Use these insights to refine your approach.

Taking these steps will help you find a niche that not only excites you but also has the potential to attract a dedicated audience. Remember, your niche is the foundation of your YouTube channel. Get this right, and you're well on your way to creating content that people will love and come back for.

And hey, don't stress too much about getting it perfect from the start. Many successful YouTubers have evolved and refined their niches over time. The important thing is to start creating and let your niche naturally develop as you gain more experience and feedback from your audience.

So, grab your camera (or smartphone), start brainstorming, and get ready to carve out your unique space in the YouTube universe. Your niche is waiting for you—go find it!

Chapter 2: Planning Your Channel

Now that you've found your niche, it's time to get organized and plan your channel. Think of this chapter as your strategic blueprint, your master plan for creating compelling content that will keep viewers coming back for more. Planning might sound a bit dull, but trust me, it's where the magic starts. Let's dive in!

Defining Your Channel's Purpose

First things first, let's define the purpose of your channel. This is your "why." Why are you making these videos? What do you hope to achieve? Defining your channel's purpose helps you stay focused and gives your content a clear direction.

Ask yourself a few questions:

What value do I want to provide to my viewers?
   What problems am I helping to solve?
   What kind of community do I want to build?
   For example, if your niche is fitness, your purpose might be to help people achieve their health goals through easy-to-follow workout routines and nutritional advice. If you're into gaming, maybe your purpose is to entertain and provide tips on mastering different games.

CHAPTER 2: PLANNING YOUR CHANNEL

Having a clear purpose not only helps you create content that's meaningful and engaging but also attracts viewers who are looking for exactly what you're offering.

Creating a Content Plan

Alright, you've got your purpose nailed down. Now let's talk content. A content plan is your roadmap to consistency, which is key to growing your channel. It's about brainstorming video ideas, organizing them, and scheduling them so you always have fresh content ready to go.

Start by brainstorming a list of video ideas. Don't censor yourself—write down everything that comes to mind. These ideas don't have to be perfect; they just need to get you started. Once you've got a decent list, start organizing these ideas into categories. For instance, if your channel is about cooking, your categories might include breakfast recipes, dinner ideas, quick snacks, and cooking tips.

Next, create a content calendar. This doesn't have to be anything fancy. A simple spreadsheet or a calendar app will do. Plan out when you'll film, edit, and publish each video. Having a schedule helps you stay on track and ensures you're consistently putting out content, which is crucial for keeping your audience engaged.

Understanding Your Target Audience

To make content that resonates, you need to understand your target audience. Who are they? What do they like? What problems are they facing that you can help solve? Knowing your audience helps you tailor your content to meet their needs and interests.

Start by creating a profile of your ideal viewer. Think about their age, gender, interests, and online behavior. Are they teenagers looking for makeup tutorials? Busy parents searching for quick and healthy meal ideas? Tech enthusiasts eager for the latest gadget reviews? The more specific you can be, the better.

Once you have a clear picture of your target audience, you can start creating content that speaks directly to them. This not only makes your videos more relevant but also helps you build a loyal community of viewers who feel like you understand them.

Branding Basics

Your brand is what sets you apart from other channels. It's how people recognize and remember you. Effective branding includes your channel name, logo, color scheme, and overall aesthetic. Let's break it down.

First, choose a channel name. It should be catchy, easy to remember, and reflective of your content. Avoid overly complicated names or ones that are too similar to existing channels. You want something that stands out.

Next, design a logo. This doesn't need to be a masterpiece, but it should be professional-looking and consistent with your channel's theme. There are plenty of free tools online like Canva that can help you create a simple yet effective logo.

Then, think about your color scheme and overall aesthetic. Consistency is key here. Use the same colors and style across your channel art, thumbnails, and videos. This creates a cohesive look that helps viewers instantly recognize your content.

Finally, write a compelling channel description. This is your chance to tell potential viewers what your channel is all about and why they should subscribe. Be clear, concise, and let your personality shine through. Mention your upload schedule if you have one, so viewers know when to expect new content.

CHAPTER 2: PLANNING YOUR CHANNEL

Channel Design

Now that you've got your branding sorted, it's time to design your channel. This involves setting up your channel layout and creating engaging visuals that attract viewers.

Start with your channel art. This includes your banner and profile picture. Your banner should be visually appealing and give viewers a sense of what your channel is about. Include your logo and maybe a tagline or upload schedule. Your profile picture should be clear and recognizable. It's often best to use a high-quality photo of yourself or your logo.

Next, organize your channel layout. YouTube allows you to customize your channel homepage with different sections. Use these sections to showcase your best content. You can create sections for your latest uploads, popular videos, and specific playlists. This helps new visitors quickly find your best work and encourages them to subscribe.

Writing a Killer Channel Description

Your channel description is one of the first things people see when they visit your channel. It's your chance to make a great first impression. Here's how to write a killer description:

Start with a Hook: Grab their attention right away. You might start with a question, a bold statement, or a fun fact about your channel.

Tell Your Story: Share a bit about who you are and why you started your channel. Let your personality shine through.

Highlight Your Content: Explain what kind of videos you make and what viewers can expect. Be clear and specific.

Include Keywords: Think about what terms people might search for to find your content. Include these keywords naturally in your description.

Call to Action: Encourage viewers to subscribe, follow you on social media, or check out your website.

Initial Video Uploads

Your first few videos are crucial. They set the tone for your channel and give new viewers a taste of what you have to offer. Here are some tips for your initial uploads:

Introduce Yourself: Start with an introductory video where you introduce yourself and your channel. Tell viewers what they can expect and why they should subscribe.

Showcase Your Best Content: Pick topics you're passionate about and that you think will resonate with your target audience. Your first few videos should be high-quality and representative of the kind of content you'll be making.

Be Consistent: Aim to upload a few videos in quick succession to give viewers a reason to stick around. Consistency helps build momentum and encourages viewers to subscribe.

Takeaways

Alright, let's sum up the key points and actionable steps to help you plan your channel:

Define Your Purpose: Know why you're making videos and what you want to achieve. This gives your content direction and meaning.

Create a Content Plan: Brainstorm video ideas, organize them into categories, and set up a content calendar to stay consistent.

Understand Your Audience: Know who your viewers are and what they want. Tailor your content to meet their needs and interests.

Brand Your Channel: Choose a catchy name, design a logo, and create a consistent aesthetic. This makes your channel recognizable and memorable.

Design Your Channel Layout: Use sections to showcase your best content and make it easy for viewers to find what they're looking for.

Write a Compelling Description: Hook viewers with a great description that tells your story, highlights your content, and includes keywords.

Plan Your Initial Uploads: Start strong with high-quality videos that represent your channel. Be consistent to build momentum.

With a solid plan in place, you're well on your way to creating a successful YouTube channel. Remember, planning might not be the most glamorous part of the process, but it's the foundation that sets you up for success. Now, let's move on to the next exciting step: creating high-quality content that your viewers will love!

Chapter 3: Setting Up Your Channel

Alright, now that you've found your niche and mapped out your plan, it's time to roll up your sleeves and set up your YouTube channel. Think of this as building your online home. You want it to be welcoming, organized, and reflective of your unique style. So, let's get down to business and make sure your channel is ready to impress.

Technical Setup

First things first, let's get the technical setup out of the way. If you haven't already created a YouTube account, now's the time. Head over to YouTube and sign in with your Google account. If you don't have one, creating a Google account is a breeze and will give you access to all of Google's services, including YouTube.

Once you're signed in, click on your profile icon in the top right corner and select "Create a Channel." You'll be prompted to choose between using your name or creating a custom name for your channel. For most YouTubers, a custom name that reflects their brand or niche is the way to go. Choose something catchy, memorable, and relevant to your content.

Navigating YouTube Studio

Welcome to YouTube Studio, your new best friend. YouTube Studio is the control center for your channel. It's where you'll upload videos, manage comments, track performance, and much more. Spend some time exploring the different sections so you get comfortable with the layout.

Here's a quick rundown of what you'll find:

Dashboard: This is your home base. It gives you an overview of your channel's performance, recent activity, and important updates from YouTube.

Content: This is where you'll manage your videos. You can see all your uploads, edit video details, and track their performance.

Analytics: Dive into the numbers here. You'll find detailed statistics on your views, watch time, audience demographics, and more.

Comments: Manage all your comments in one place. You can reply, like, or delete comments, and even filter them to find the ones that need your attention.

Customization: Here's where you'll personalize your channel's look and feel. You can edit your channel layout, branding, and basic info.

Channel Design

Now that you're familiar with YouTube Studio, let's make your channel look professional and appealing. Your channel design includes your profile picture, banner, and overall layout.

Start with your profile picture. This should be a high-quality image that represents you or your brand. If you're the face of your channel, a clear, friendly headshot is a great choice. If your channel is more about your brand, use your logo.

Next up is your banner. This is the large image that spans the top of your channel page. It's prime real estate for showcasing your brand and giving new visitors a sense of what your channel is all about. Your banner should include your logo, a tagline or brief description, and possibly your upload schedule. Use a design tool like Canva to create a professional-looking banner that fits YouTube's dimensions (2560 x 1440 pixels).

Organizing your channel layout is also crucial. YouTube allows you to customize your channel homepage with different sections. Use these sections to highlight your best content. For example, you can create sections for your latest uploads, popular videos, and specific playlists related to different topics within your niche. This helps visitors quickly find your best work and encourages them to explore more of your content.

Writing a Killer Channel Description

Your channel description is your elevator pitch. It's your chance to tell visitors what your channel is about and why they should subscribe. Here's how to craft a compelling description:

Start with a Hook: Grab their attention right away with an interesting fact, a question, or a bold statement.

Introduce Yourself: Share a bit about who you are and why you started your channel. Let your personality shine through.

Highlight Your Content: Explain what kind of videos you make and what viewers can expect. Be clear and specific.

Include Keywords: Think about the terms people might use to search for your content. Include these keywords naturally in your description to help your channel get discovered.

Call to Action: Encourage viewers to subscribe, follow you on social media, or check out your website.

Initial Video Uploads

Your first few videos set the tone for your channel and give new visitors a taste of what to expect. Here are some tips for your initial uploads:

Introduce Yourself: Start with a welcome video where you introduce yourself and your channel. Share your story and what inspired you to start your channel. This helps viewers connect with you on a personal level.

Showcase Your Best Content: Pick topics you're passionate about and that you think will resonate with your target audience. Your first few videos should be high-quality and representative of the kind of content you'll be making.

Be Consistent: Aim to upload a few videos in quick succession to give viewers a reason to stick around. Consistency helps build momentum and encourages viewers to subscribe.

Optimize Your Videos: Make sure your video titles, descriptions, and tags are optimized for search. This helps your videos get discovered by new viewers.

Creating Engaging Thumbnails and Titles

Your thumbnails and titles are the first things potential viewers see, so they need to be eye-catching and enticing. Here's how to create thumbnails and titles that get clicks:

Thumbnails: Use high-quality images with bright, contrasting colors. Include text to highlight the main point of your video, but keep it short and readable. Make sure your thumbnails are consistent in style to create a cohesive look for your channel.

Titles: Be clear and specific about what your video is about. Use keywords that people are likely to search for. Create a sense of curiosity or urgency to encourage viewers to click.

Engaging with Your Community

Building a loyal community is essential for your channel's growth. Engage with your viewers by responding to comments, asking for feedback, and creating a sense of belonging. Here are some tips:

Reply to Comments: Take the time to respond to comments on your videos. Thank viewers for their feedback, answer questions, and engage in conversations. This shows that you value your audience and are interested in what they have to say.

Ask for Feedback: Encourage viewers to share their thoughts and suggestions. This not only helps you improve your content but also makes viewers feel like they're part of the process.

Create Community Posts: Use YouTube's Community tab to share updates, polls, and behind-the-scenes content. This keeps your audience engaged between video uploads and helps build a stronger connection.

Analyzing Your Performance

Once you start uploading videos, it's important to track their performance. This helps you understand what's working and what's not, so you can continuously improve your content. Here are some key metrics to monitor:

Views: The number of times your video has been watched. This gives you a general idea of its popularity.

Watch Time: The total amount of time viewers have spent watching your video.

This metric is crucial because YouTube's algorithm favors videos with higher watch times.

Audience Retention: The percentage of viewers who watch your video from start to finish. High retention rates indicate that your content is engaging and keeps viewers hooked.

Engagement: The number of likes, comments, and shares your video receives. High engagement signals that your content resonates with your audience.

Subscriber Growth: The number of new subscribers you gain from each video. This helps you understand which types of content attract new viewers.

Adjusting Your Strategy

Based on your performance data, you might need to adjust your content strategy. Here's how to use your analytics to make informed decisions:

Identify Trends: Look for patterns in your data. Which videos have the highest views, watch time, and engagement? What do these videos have in common?

Experiment: Try different types of content, formats, and topics to see what resonates with your audience. Don't be afraid to take risks and try new things.

Optimize: Use your findings to optimize future videos. For example, if you notice that videos with certain keywords or thumbnails perform better, incorporate those elements into your next uploads.

Listen to Your Audience: Pay attention to viewer feedback and adjust your content accordingly. Your audience's input is invaluable for improving your channel.

Takeaways

To wrap up, let's summarize the key points from this chapter:

Technical Setup: Create your YouTube account, navigate YouTube Studio, and get familiar with the different sections.

Channel Design: Choose a high-quality profile picture, create an eye-catching banner, and organize your channel layout.

Channel Description: Write a compelling description that hooks viewers, introduces yourself, highlights your content, includes keywords, and has a call to action.

Initial Video Uploads: Start with an introduction video, showcase your best content, be consistent, and optimize your videos for search.

Thumbnails and Titles: Create eye-catching thumbnails and clear, enticing titles to attract viewers.

Engage with Your Community: Respond to comments, ask for feedback, and use community posts to keep your audience engaged.

Analyze Performance: Monitor key metrics like views, watch time, audience retention, engagement, and subscriber growth.

Adjust Strategy: Use your analytics to identify trends, experiment with different content, optimize future videos, and listen to your audience.

Setting up your channel might seem like a lot of work, but it's the foundation of your YouTube journey. A well-organized and visually appealing channel attracts viewers and keeps them coming back for more. So take your time, get creative, and make your channel the best it can be. Next up, we'll dive into creating high-quality content that will captivate your audience.

Chapter 4: Creating High-Quality Content

Congratulations on setting up your YouTube channel! Now comes the fun part—creating high-quality content that will captivate your audience and keep them coming back for more. This chapter is all about the nuts and bolts of video production, from filming techniques to editing magic. Let's roll up our sleeves and dive into the world of content creation.

Video Production Basics

Before you start filming, you need to gather your tools. Don't worry, you don't need a Hollywood budget to create great videos. Here's a rundown of the essential equipment:

Camera: Your smartphone can be a great starting point. Modern smartphones have excellent cameras that can shoot in high resolution. If you're ready to invest a bit more, consider a DSLR or a mirrorless camera for even better quality and more control over your shots.

Microphone: Good audio is crucial. Viewers might forgive a slightly blurry video, but poor audio quality is a dealbreaker. An external microphone, like a lavalier (clip-on) mic or a shotgun mic, can significantly improve your sound.

Lighting: Natural light is your friend, but it can be unpredictable. A basic lighting setup with a couple of softbox lights or ring lights can make a big difference in the quality of your videos. Position your lights to eliminate shadows and create a bright, even look.

Tripod: A stable shot is a professional shot. Use a tripod to keep your camera steady and avoid shaky footage. There are affordable options available for both smartphones and cameras.

Filming Techniques

Now that you've got your gear, let's talk about filming techniques. Even if you have the best equipment, knowing how to use it effectively is key to producing high-quality content.

Framing: Pay attention to how you frame your shots. Use the rule of thirds to create balanced and visually appealing compositions. Imagine your screen is divided into nine equal parts by two horizontal and two vertical lines. Place your subject along these lines or at their intersections.

Focus: Make sure your subject is in focus. Blurry footage can be distracting and unprofessional. If you're using a smartphone, tap on the screen to focus on your subject. With a camera, use manual focus if necessary.

Stability: Keep your shots steady. If you're filming handheld, try to keep your movements smooth and avoid sudden jerks. A tripod or a stabilizer can help you achieve more professional-looking footage.

Angles: Experiment with different angles to add variety to your videos. Don't be afraid to get creative. High angles, low angles, and side shots can make your content more dynamic and interesting.

Editing Your Videos

Editing is where the magic happens. It's your chance to polish your footage,

CHAPTER 4: CREATING HIGH-QUALITY CONTENT

add effects, and create a cohesive story. Here's a step-by-step guide to basic video editing:

Choose Your Software: There are plenty of editing software options out there, from free tools like iMovie and DaVinci Resolve to professional software like Adobe Premiere Pro and Final Cut Pro. Choose one that fits your budget and skill level.

Import Your Footage: Start by importing your footage into your editing software. Organize your clips in a logical order so you can easily find what you need.

Cut and Trim: Go through your footage and cut out any unnecessary parts. Trim the beginning and end of each clip to remove any awkward pauses or mistakes. Your goal is to create a smooth, engaging flow.

Add Transitions: Use transitions to smoothly connect your clips. Simple cuts are usually the best, but you can also experiment with fades and dissolves. Avoid overusing flashy transitions—they can be distracting.

Include Music and Sound Effects: Background music can enhance your video and set the mood. Choose music that fits the tone of your content and make sure it's not too loud. Sound effects can also add a professional touch.

Color Correction: Adjust the color and brightness of your footage to make it look more polished. Most editing software includes basic color correction tools. Aim for natural, well-balanced colors.

Add Text and Graphics: Text overlays and graphics can highlight important information and make your videos more engaging. Use them sparingly and make sure they're easy to read.

Thumbnails and Titles

Your thumbnails and titles are the first things viewers see, so they need to grab attention. Here's how to create compelling thumbnails and titles:

Thumbnails: Use high-quality images with bright, contrasting colors. Include text to highlight the main point of your video, but keep it short and readable. Make sure your thumbnails are consistent in style to create a cohesive look for your channel.

Titles: Be clear and specific about what your video is about. Use keywords that people are likely to search for. Create a sense of curiosity or urgency to encourage viewers to click.

Scripting Your Videos

Having a script can make a huge difference in the quality of your videos. It helps you stay organized, cover all the points you want to make, and keep your videos concise. Here's how to write an effective script:

Outline Your Content: Start with an outline of the main points you want to cover. This helps you structure your video and ensures you don't miss anything important.

Write Conversationally: Write your script in a conversational tone, as if you're speaking directly to your viewers. This makes your videos more engaging and relatable.

Keep It Short and Sweet: Aim for brevity. People's attention spans are short, so get to the point quickly and avoid unnecessary rambling.

Include Call to Actions: Encourage viewers to like, comment, and subscribe. Ask them questions to engage them and get them involved in the conversation.

Engaging Your Audience

Engagement is key to building a loyal audience. Here are some tips to keep your viewers coming back for more:

Be Authentic: Let your personality shine through. People connect with authenticity, so be yourself and don't try to be someone you're not.

Tell Stories: Stories are powerful. They capture attention and make your content more memorable. Share personal anecdotes or interesting stories related to your topic.

Ask Questions: Engage your audience by asking questions and encouraging them to leave comments. This not only increases engagement but also gives you valuable feedback.

Respond to Comments: Take the time to respond to comments on your videos. This shows your viewers that you value their input and appreciate their support.

Collaborating with Other YouTubers

Collaborations can help you reach a wider audience and add variety to your content. Here's how to find and approach potential collaborators:

Find Channels in Your Niche: Look for other YouTubers who create content similar to yours. Check out their videos and see if their style and audience align with yours.

Reach Out: Send a friendly, personalized message introducing yourself and suggesting a collaboration. Be clear about what you have in mind and how it will benefit both channels.

Plan Your Collaboration: Once you've found a collaborator, plan your content together. Decide on the format, topics, and how you'll promote each other's channels.

Promote the Collaboration: Share the collaboration on your social media and encourage your viewers to check out your collaborator's channel. Cross-promotion helps both channels grow.

Staying Consistent

Consistency is crucial for growing your channel. Here are some tips to stay consistent with your uploads:

Set a Schedule: Decide on a realistic upload schedule and stick to it. Whether it's once a week or twice a month, consistency helps build anticipation and keeps your audience engaged.

Batch Filming: Film multiple videos in one session. This saves time and ensures you always have content ready to go, even when life gets busy.

Stay Organized: Keep a content calendar and plan your videos in advance. This helps you stay on track and avoid last-minute scrambling.

Take Breaks When Needed: It's important to take breaks to avoid burnout. Communicate with your audience if you need to take a break, and let them know when you'll be back.

Takeaways

Let's recap the key points from this chapter:

Gather Your Tools: Invest in essential equipment like a good camera, microphone, lighting, and a tripod.

Master Filming Techniques: Pay attention to framing, focus, stability, and angles to create professional-looking footage.

Edit Like a Pro: Use editing software to cut and trim your footage, add transitions, music, and text, and perform color correction.

Create Engaging Thumbnails and Titles: Use high-quality images, bright colors, and clear, enticing titles to attract viewers.

Write Effective Scripts: Outline your content, write conversationally, keep it concise, and include calls to action.

Engage Your Audience: Be authentic, tell stories, ask questions, and respond to comments to build a loyal community.

Collaborate with Others: Find channels in your niche, reach out, plan collaborations, and promote each other's content.

Stay Consistent: Set a realistic upload schedule, batch film, stay organized, and take breaks when needed.

Creating high-quality content is the heart of your YouTube channel. It's what keeps viewers coming back and helps you build a loyal audience. With these tips and techniques, you're well on your way to producing videos that stand out and resonate with your viewers. Now, let's move on to the next exciting chapter: optimizing your content for search and discovery.

Chapter 5: Optimizing for Search and Discovery

Welcome to the fascinating world of YouTube SEO. Think of this chapter as your guide to getting noticed. You've got great content, but what good is it if no one sees it? That's where search and discovery optimization comes in. By the end of this chapter, you'll understand how to make your videos more discoverable, so viewers can find and fall in love with your content. Let's dive into the nitty-gritty of YouTube SEO.

Understanding YouTube SEO

SEO, or Search Engine Optimization, might sound like techy jargon, but it's simpler than you think. SEO is all about making sure your videos appear in search results when people are looking for content like yours. It's how you go from being an invisible needle in a digital haystack to a bright, shiny pin that everyone wants to find.

On YouTube, SEO involves optimizing various elements of your video to improve its visibility. These elements include your video's title, description, tags, and even the content itself. When done right, SEO can help your videos rank higher in search results, attract more viewers, and grow your channel faster.

CHAPTER 5: OPTIMIZING FOR SEARCH AND DISCOVERY

Optimizing Your Video Metadata

Let's start with the basics: your video metadata. This includes your title, description, and tags. Think of metadata as the "packaging" of your video—it's what viewers see first and what search engines use to understand your content.

Titles: Your video title is the first thing people see, and it plays a crucial role in determining whether they'll click on your video. Make sure your title is clear, concise, and includes relevant keywords. Keywords are the terms people are likely to use when searching for content like yours. For example, if your video is about baking chocolate chip cookies, a good title might be "How to Bake Perfect Chocolate Chip Cookies."

Descriptions: Your video description is an opportunity to provide more context about your content. Use the first few lines to summarize the video and include important keywords. Beyond that, you can add more details, links to related content, and even timestamps to help viewers navigate your video. A well-crafted description not only helps with SEO but also enhances the viewer's experience.

Tags: Tags are another way to signal to YouTube what your video is about. Use a mix of broad and specific tags to cover all the bases. For our chocolate chip cookie video, you might use tags like "baking," "cookies," "chocolate chip cookies," and "dessert recipes." Don't go overboard with tags—focus on quality over quantity.

Engaging Thumbnails

Your thumbnail is like a movie poster for your video. It needs to grab attention and entice viewers to click. High-quality, engaging thumbnails can significantly boost your click-through rate (CTR), which in turn improves your video's ranking.

Here are some tips for creating effective thumbnails:

Use High-Resolution Images: Blurry, pixelated thumbnails are a no-go. Make sure your thumbnail is clear and high-quality.

Bright, Contrasting Colors: Thumbnails with bright, contrasting colors stand out in search results and on the sidebar.

Include Text: Adding a few words to your thumbnail can highlight the video's main point and attract clicks. Just keep it short and readable.

Consistent Branding: Use similar styles, colors, and fonts for all your thumbnails to create a cohesive look across your channel.

Playlists and Series

Playlists are a fantastic tool for increasing watch time and keeping viewers engaged with your content. By organizing your videos into playlists, you can guide viewers to watch multiple videos in a row, boosting your overall watch time and improving your SEO.

Create playlists around specific themes or series. For example, if you have a cooking channel, you could create playlists for different types of cuisine, like "Italian Recipes," "Dessert Ideas," or "Healthy Meals." Not only do playlists make it easier for viewers to find related content, but they also improve your chances of showing up in search results and suggested videos.

Understanding Watch Time and Audience Retention

YouTube's algorithm loves watch time. The more time people spend watching your videos, the more likely YouTube is to promote your content. This means that keeping viewers engaged is crucial for your channel's success.

Audience retention measures how long viewers stay engaged with your video. High audience retention indicates that people find your content valuable and interesting, which is a big plus for your SEO. Here's how to improve your watch time and audience retention:

Start Strong: Grab viewers' attention in the first few seconds. Use a hook, like an intriguing question, a surprising fact, or a quick preview of what's coming up in the video.

Keep It Pacing: Avoid long, drawn-out introductions and get to the point quickly. Keep the content moving to maintain interest.

Use Engaging Visuals: Mix things up with different camera angles, cutaway shots, and graphics to keep the visual interest high.

End with a Teaser: At the end of your video, tease your next video to encourage viewers to come back for more.

Promoting Your Channel

Optimization doesn't stop with YouTube. Promoting your videos across different platforms can drive more traffic to your channel and improve your SEO. Here are some effective ways to promote your channel:

Social Media: Share your videos on social media platforms like Facebook, Twitter, Instagram, and LinkedIn. Tailor your posts to fit the style of each platform and engage with your followers.

Blog Posts: If you have a blog, write articles related to your video content and embed your videos. This not only drives traffic from your blog to your YouTube channel but also helps with SEO.

Email Newsletters: If you have an email list, send out newsletters with links to your latest videos. Encourage your subscribers to watch, like, and share your content.

Collaborations: Partner with other YouTubers in your niche. Collaboration exposes your channel to a new audience and can significantly boost your subscriber count.

Cross-Promote: Mention your videos and channel in other content you create, such as podcasts, webinars, or online courses.

Using YouTube Analytics

To optimize your content effectively, you need to understand how your videos are performing. YouTube Analytics provides valuable insights into your audience's behavior and helps you identify what's working and what's not.

Here are some key metrics to track:

Views: The number of times your video has been watched. This gives you a general idea of your video's popularity.

Watch Time: The total amount of time viewers have spent watching your video. Higher watch time indicates more engaged viewers.

Audience Retention: The percentage of viewers who watch your video from start to finish. High retention rates are a positive signal to YouTube's algorithm.

CTR (Click-Through Rate): The percentage of people who clicked on your video after seeing the thumbnail. A higher CTR means your thumbnails and titles are effective.

Traffic Sources: Where your viewers are coming from, such as search results, suggested videos, or external websites. Understanding your traffic sources helps you focus your promotion efforts.

Use these insights to refine your strategy, improve your content, and optimize future videos for even better performance.

Adjusting Your Strategy

SEO is not a set-it-and-forget-it task. It requires continuous monitoring and tweaking. Based on your analytics, you might need to adjust your strategy.

Here's how to stay on top of your SEO game:

Monitor Performance: Regularly check your YouTube Analytics to see how your videos are performing. Look for patterns and trends to understand what types of content resonate with your audience.

Experiment: Don't be afraid to try new things. Experiment with different types of content, formats, and promotion strategies to see what works best.

Optimize Titles and Descriptions: Based on your performance data, tweak your video titles and descriptions to improve their effectiveness.

Engage with Your Audience: Pay attention to comments and feedback. Use viewer suggestions to improve your content and make it more relevant to your audience.

Stay Updated: SEO best practices can change over time. Stay updated with the latest trends and algorithm changes to keep your channel optimized.

Takeaways

Optimizing your videos for search and discovery is crucial for growing your YouTube channel. By focusing on SEO, you can improve your visibility, attract more viewers, and build a loyal audience.

Here's a quick recap of the key points:

Understand YouTube SEO: Make your videos discoverable by optimizing titles, descriptions, and tags.

Create Engaging Thumbnails: Use high-quality images, bright colors, and text to attract clicks.

Use Playlists: Organize your videos into playlists to increase watch time and engagement.

Improve Watch Time: Keep viewers engaged with strong starts, engaging visuals, and teasers for future content.

Promote Your Channel: Share your videos on social media, blogs, and through collaborations to drive traffic.

Analyze and Adjust: Use YouTube Analytics to track performance and refine your strategy.

By following these tips and continuously optimizing your content, you'll increase your chances of being discovered and grow your YouTube channel faster. Now, let's move on to the next chapter, where we'll discuss how to grow your audience and keep them coming back for more.

Chapter 6: Growing Your Audience

Alright, you've got your channel set up and some high-quality content ready to go. Now, it's time to tackle one of the biggest challenges every YouTuber faces: growing your audience. It's one thing to have a few viewers trickle in, but how do you turn that trickle into a steady stream? How do you build a community of loyal fans who eagerly await your next video? Let's dive into some strategies to help you grow your audience and create a thriving YouTube channel.

Promoting Your Channel

To grow your audience, you need to get your channel in front of as many eyes as possible. Promotion is key, and there are several effective ways to do it.

Social Media: Leveraging social media platforms is a must. Share your videos on Facebook, Twitter, Instagram, and LinkedIn. Tailor your posts to fit the style of each platform. For instance, Instagram is great for behind-the-scenes shots and short clips, while Twitter can be used for quick updates and engaging with your audience.

Cross-Promotion: Collaborate with other YouTubers in your niche. Cross-promotion exposes your channel to a new audience. Reach out to creators whose content complements yours and propose collaboration ideas. This could be anything from guest appearances to co-hosting a series of videos.

Forums and Communities: Participate in online forums and communities related to your niche. Platforms like Reddit and specialized forums can be great places to share your content and engage with potential viewers. Just remember to follow the community guidelines and avoid spamming.

SEO and Keywords: We've touched on SEO in previous chapters, but it's worth reiterating. Use relevant keywords in your titles, descriptions, and tags to improve your searchability. This will help people discover your videos through search engines and YouTube's own search function.

Engaging with Your Community

Building a loyal audience goes beyond just getting views; it's about creating a community. Engaging with your viewers makes them feel valued and connected to you.

Respond to Comments: Take the time to reply to comments on your videos. Thank viewers for their feedback, answer questions, and engage in conversations. This not only shows appreciation but also encourages more people to comment.

Ask for Feedback: Encourage your viewers to share their thoughts and suggestions. This makes them feel involved and gives you valuable insights into what they enjoy and what they'd like to see more of.

Create Community Posts: Use YouTube's Community tab to interact with your audience. Share updates, polls, and behind-the-scenes content. This keeps your audience engaged between video uploads and fosters a sense of belonging.

Host Live Streams: Live streaming is a fantastic way to engage with your audience in real-time. Host Q&A sessions, behind-the-scenes tours, or even casual hangouts. Live interactions help build a deeper connection with your viewers.

Analyzing Your Performance

Growing your audience involves understanding what works and what doesn't. YouTube Analytics is your best friend in this endeavor. It provides detailed insights into your channel's performance and helps you make data-driven decisions.

Key Metrics to Track:

Views: The number of times your video has been watched. This gives you a general idea of its popularity.

Watch Time: The total amount of time viewers have spent watching your videos. Higher watch time indicates more engaged viewers.

Audience Retention: The percentage of viewers who watch your video from start to finish. High retention rates suggest your content is engaging.

Engagement: The number of likes, comments, and shares your videos receive. High engagement signals that your content resonates with your audience.

Subscriber Growth: The number of new subscribers you gain over time. This helps you understand which types of content attract new viewers.

Use these insights to refine your content strategy. Identify which videos perform the best and analyze what makes them successful. Experiment with different formats, topics, and styles to see what resonates most with your audience.

Building a Consistent Upload Schedule

Consistency is crucial for audience growth. Viewers are more likely to subscribe and stick around if they know when to expect new content from you.

Create a Content Calendar: Plan your videos in advance and stick to a regular upload schedule. Whether it's once a week or twice a month, consistency helps build anticipation and keeps your audience engaged.

Batch Filming: Consider filming multiple videos in one session. This saves time and ensures you always have content ready to go, even when life gets busy.

Communicate with Your Audience: Let your viewers know your upload schedule. Mention it in your videos, include it in your channel description, and stick to it as much as possible.

Quality over Quantity: While consistency is important, don't sacrifice quality for the sake of posting frequently. It's better to upload high-quality content less often than to post mediocre videos regularly.

Creating Engaging Content

Ultimately, the best way to grow your audience is to create content that people love. Here are some tips for making engaging videos:

Tell a Story: People love stories. Whether it's a personal anecdote, a step-by-step process, or a journey, structuring your videos like a story keeps viewers hooked.

Be Authentic: Let your personality shine through. Authenticity builds trust and makes your content more relatable.

Use Visuals: Enhance your videos with engaging visuals. This could be graphics, animations, or simply different camera angles. Visual variety keeps viewers interested.

Include a Call to Action: Encourage viewers to like, comment, and subscribe. Ask questions to engage them and get them involved in the conversation.

CHAPTER 6: GROWING YOUR AUDIENCE

Experiment and Innovate: Don't be afraid to try new things. Experiment with different video formats, styles, and topics to see what resonates with your audience.

Leveraging Trends

Keeping up with trends can give your channel a significant boost. Here's how to leverage trends to grow your audience:

Stay Updated: Keep an eye on current trends in your niche and the wider YouTube community. Tools like Google Trends and YouTube's trending page can help you stay informed.

Create Timely Content: When you spot a trend that fits your channel, create content around it quickly. Timely videos are more likely to get noticed and shared.

Put Your Spin on It: Don't just copy what others are doing. Put your unique spin on the trend to make your content stand out.

Collaborate with Influencers: Collaborating with influencers who are riding a trend can expose your channel to a larger audience.

Encouraging Subscriptions

Subscribers are the lifeblood of your channel. They are your most loyal viewers who are likely to watch, like, and share your videos. Here's how to encourage more people to subscribe:

Ask Directly: Sometimes, all you need to do is ask. At the end of your videos, remind viewers to subscribe and explain why it's beneficial for them.

Offer Incentives: Give viewers a reason to subscribe. This could be exclusive content, early access to videos, or special giveaways.

Highlight the Benefits: Clearly communicate the benefits of subscribing. For example, subscribers get notified about new videos, special live streams, and exclusive content.

Engage with Subscribers: Show appreciation to your subscribers by engaging with them regularly. Respond to their comments, mention them in videos, and create content based on their suggestions.

Takeaways

Growing your audience on YouTube is a multifaceted endeavor that involves promotion, engagement, analysis, and consistency. By implementing these strategies, you can attract more viewers, build a loyal community, and create a thriving channel.

Promote Your Channel: Use social media, cross-promotion, and SEO to get your content in front of more eyes.

Engage with Your Community: Respond to comments, ask for feedback, and use live streams to build a deeper connection with your viewers.

Analyze Performance: Use YouTube Analytics to track key metrics and refine your content strategy.

Maintain Consistency: Stick to a regular upload schedule and communicate it with your audience.

Create Engaging Content: Tell stories, be authentic, use visuals, and include calls to action to keep viewers hooked.

Leverage Trends: Stay updated with trends and create timely content that resonates with your audience.

Encourage Subscriptions: Ask viewers to subscribe, offer incentives, and highlight the benefits of subscribing.

With these strategies, you're well on your way to growing a dedicated audience and making your mark on YouTube.

Chapter 7: Monetization Strategies

You've put in the hard work, created engaging content, and started building a loyal audience. Now, it's time to talk about something that's probably been on your mind since you first hit the record button: making money from your YouTube channel. Monetization might seem like a distant dream when you're just starting out, but with the right strategies, you can turn your passion into a source of income. Let's dive into the various monetization strategies available and how you can make the most of them.

YouTube Partner Program

The YouTube Partner Program (YPP) is the most straightforward way to start earning money from your channel. To join YPP, you need to meet certain requirements: have at least 1,000 subscribers and 4,000 watch hours over the past 12 months. Once you've reached these milestones, you can apply for the program through YouTube Studio.

Ad Revenue: The primary way YouTubers earn money through YPP is via ad revenue. Advertisers pay YouTube to run ads on videos, and YouTube shares a percentage of that revenue with creators. The amount you earn depends on factors like the number of views, viewer demographics, and ad engagement.

Super Chat and Super Stickers: If you host live streams, Super Chat and Super Stickers are fantastic ways to earn money. Viewers can purchase these features to highlight their messages or send animated stickers during your live streams. It's a great way to make your live sessions more interactive and profitable.

Channel Memberships: Once you're part of YPP, you can offer channel memberships. For a monthly fee, members get perks like exclusive badges, emojis, and members-only content. It's a way to offer more value to your most dedicated fans while earning a steady income.

Ad Revenue

Ad revenue is the bread and butter of many YouTube channels, but it's not as simple as just turning on ads. Here are some tips to maximize your earnings from ad revenue:

Create Longer Videos: YouTube favors longer videos when it comes to ad placement. Videos over 10 minutes can include multiple ad breaks, increasing your revenue potential. Just make sure the content remains engaging and doesn't drag on unnecessarily.

Optimize Ad Placement: You can choose where ads appear in your videos—before, during, or after. Mid-roll ads (ads that appear in the middle of the video) can be particularly effective, especially for longer videos. Experiment with different placements to see what works best for your audience.

Engage Your Audience: High viewer engagement can lead to better ad performance. Encourage likes, comments, and shares to boost your video's engagement metrics, which can, in turn, improve ad revenue.

Alternative Revenue Streams

While ad revenue is significant, relying solely on it can be limiting. Diversifying your income streams can provide more financial stability and potentially higher earnings. Here are some alternative revenue streams to consider:

CHAPTER 7: MONETIZATION STRATEGIES

Sponsorships: Brands are always looking to collaborate with influencers who align with their products or services. Reach out to companies that fit your niche or use platforms like FameBit or Grapevine to find sponsorship opportunities. Sponsored videos typically involve you promoting a product or service in exchange for payment.

Affiliate Marketing: Promote products or services in your videos and include affiliate links in your description. When viewers purchase through your link, you earn a commission. This works well if you genuinely believe in the products you're promoting. Amazon Associates is a popular affiliate program to start with, but there are many others depending on your niche.

Merchandise: Selling your own merchandise can be a lucrative way to monetize your channel. You can sell t-shirts, mugs, stickers, or any other products that resonate with your brand. Platforms like Teespring and Merchbar integrate with YouTube, making it easy to promote and sell your merch directly from your channel.

Crowdfunding: Platforms like Patreon and Ko-fi allow your fans to support you financially. In exchange, you can offer exclusive content, behind-the-scenes access, or other perks. Crowdfunding is a great way to earn a steady income while building a closer relationship with your most dedicated fans.

Digital Products: If you have skills or knowledge to share, consider creating digital products like e-books, online courses, or exclusive video content. These products can be sold on platforms like Gumroad or directly through your website.

Creating Paid Content

Offering paid content is another excellent way to monetize your channel. This can include creating exclusive videos for paying subscribers or offering in-depth courses on topics you're an expert in. Here are some ways to create and market paid content:

Exclusive Videos: Create special videos that only your paying subscribers can access. These could be tutorials, behind-the-scenes footage, or in-depth analysis that you don't share on your main channel. Promote these exclusive videos on your main channel to entice viewers to subscribe.

Online Courses: If you have expertise in a particular area, creating an online course can be highly profitable. Use platforms like Udemy, Skillshare, or Teachable to create and sell your courses. Online courses are especially effective if you can provide value that viewers can't get for free.

Webinars and Workshops: Host live webinars or workshops on topics of interest to your audience. Charge a fee for access and provide valuable, interactive content. Webinars are a great way to engage with your audience in real-time while earning money.

Diversifying Your Content

To maximize your earning potential, consider diversifying the types of content you create. Here are a few ideas:

How-to and Tutorial Videos: These are highly valuable and tend to attract a lot of views. If you can teach something useful, there's a good chance people will watch and share your videos.

Review and Unboxing Videos: Reviewing products or unboxing new items can attract views, especially if the products are popular or newly released. These videos also provide opportunities for affiliate marketing and sponsorships.

Vlogs and Behind-the-Scenes: Show your viewers a more personal side with vlogs or behind-the-scenes videos. These types of videos can build a stronger connection with your audience and keep them engaged.

CHAPTER 7: MONETIZATION STRATEGIES

Q&A and AMA (Ask Me Anything): Engage directly with your audience by answering their questions in a Q&A format. This not only provides valuable content but also fosters a sense of community.

Investing in Your Channel

As your channel starts to generate income, it's a good idea to reinvest some of that money back into your content. Here's how you can invest in your channel to ensure continued growth:

Upgrade Your Equipment: Better cameras, microphones, and lighting can significantly improve the quality of your videos. High-quality content attracts more viewers and keeps them engaged longer.

Outsource Tasks: As your channel grows, you might find it challenging to handle everything yourself. Consider outsourcing tasks like video editing, graphic design, or social media management to professionals. This allows you to focus on creating content while maintaining high production standards.

Marketing and Promotion: Invest in marketing your channel through paid promotions, collaborations, or hiring a marketing expert. Effective marketing can help you reach a larger audience and grow your channel faster.

Attend Conferences and Workshops: Invest in your education by attending industry conferences and workshops. These events can provide valuable insights, networking opportunities, and inspiration for your channel.

Keeping Your Audience Happy

While monetization is important, keeping your audience happy should always be your top priority. Here are some tips for maintaining a positive relationship with your viewers:

Be Transparent: If you're doing sponsored content or affiliate marketing, be upfront about it. Transparency builds trust and shows that you respect your audience.

Provide Value: Always aim to provide value in your videos. Whether it's entertainment, education, or inspiration, make sure your viewers feel like they're getting something out of your content.

Engage Regularly: Interact with your audience through comments, social media, and live streams. Show appreciation for their support and make them feel like they're part of your community.

Listen to Feedback: Pay attention to what your viewers are saying. Use their feedback to improve your content and address any concerns they might have.

Takeaways

Monetizing your YouTube channel involves a mix of strategies, from joining the YouTube Partner Program to exploring alternative revenue streams and creating paid content. Here are the key points to remember:

Join the YouTube Partner Program: Meet the requirements to start earning ad revenue, and take advantage of Super Chat, Super Stickers, and channel memberships.

Maximize Ad Revenue: Create longer videos, optimize ad placement, and engage your audience to boost earnings.

Explore Alternative Revenue Streams: Consider sponsorships, affiliate marketing, merchandise, crowdfunding, and digital products.

Offer Paid Content: Create exclusive videos, online courses, webinars, or workshops to provide additional value to your paying subscribers.

Diversify Your Content: Experiment with different types of videos to attract a broader audience and increase engagement.

Invest in Your Channel: Reinvest some of your earnings into better equipment, outsourcing tasks, marketing, and education.

Keep Your Audience Happy: Be transparent, provide value, engage regularly, and listen to feedback to maintain a positive relationship with your viewers.

By implementing these strategies, you can turn your passion for creating videos into a sustainable source of income.

Chapter 8: Legal and Ethical Considerations

You've got your channel up and running, content is flowing, and the subscribers are starting to roll in. Now, it's time to address a less glamorous but crucial aspect of being a YouTuber: legal and ethical considerations. Navigating the legal landscape and maintaining ethical standards is essential to building a trustworthy and sustainable channel. Let's dive into the key legal and ethical issues you need to be aware of and how to handle them.

Copyright Laws

Copyright is one of the most common legal issues YouTubers face. In simple terms, copyright protects the original works of creators, such as music, videos, images, and text. Using copyrighted material without permission can lead to your video being taken down, your channel receiving strikes, or even legal action.

Understand Fair Use: Fair use is a doctrine that allows limited use of copyrighted material without permission for purposes such as criticism, commentary, news reporting, teaching, scholarship, or research. However, fair use is a gray area and highly subjective. When in doubt, it's best to avoid using copyrighted material.

Use Royalty-Free Music and Images: There are plenty of sources for royalty-free music and images that you can use in your videos without worrying about copyright issues. Websites like Pixabay, Unsplash, and the YouTube Audio Library offer free resources. Always check the license terms to ensure proper use.

Create Your Own Content: The safest way to avoid copyright issues is to create your own content. This means filming your own videos, recording your own music, and designing your own graphics. It might be more work, but it ensures that your content is original and legally safe.

Seek Permission: If you want to use someone else's work, seek permission. Many creators are open to collaboration or will allow you to use their work if you give proper credit. Get the permission in writing to avoid any future disputes.

Fair Use and Creative Commons

Fair use and Creative Commons are two concepts that can help you use content legally and responsibly.

Fair Use: As mentioned earlier, fair use allows limited use of copyrighted material without permission. However, it's important to understand that fair use is determined on a case-by-case basis and considers factors like the purpose of use, the nature of the copyrighted work, the amount used, and the effect on the market value of the original work. If you're unsure whether your use qualifies as fair use, consult a legal professional.

Creative Commons: Creative Commons (CC) licenses allow creators to share their work with certain permissions already granted. For example, a CC BY license lets you use the work as long as you give appropriate credit. When using Creative Commons material, always adhere to the license terms specified by the creator.

Disclosure and Transparency

Being transparent with your audience is not just ethical; it's also a legal requirement in many cases. Here's how to maintain transparency in your content:

Sponsored Content: If you're being paid to promote a product or service, disclose it clearly. Use phrases like "This video is sponsored by..." at the beginning of the video. Many regions have regulations requiring such disclosures to prevent misleading advertising.

Affiliate Links: If you include affiliate links in your video descriptions, let your viewers know that you earn a commission from purchases made through those links. Transparency builds trust with your audience and keeps you compliant with advertising laws.

Product Reviews: When reviewing products, be honest about your opinions and disclose any relationships with the brands. If you received a product for free or were paid to review it, let your viewers know.

Conflicts of Interest: Avoid conflicts of interest that could compromise your integrity. For instance, if you're promoting a product from a company you own or have a stake in, disclose this to your audience.

Dealing with Takedown Notices

Takedown notices are legal requests to remove content that allegedly infringes on someone's copyright. Here's how to handle them:

Understand DMCA: The Digital Millennium Copyright Act (DMCA) provides a process for copyright holders to request the removal of infringing content. If you receive a DMCA takedown notice, review the claim carefully.

Responding to Takedown Notices: If you believe the takedown notice is valid, remove the infringing content to avoid further legal action. If you think the notice is incorrect or that your use qualifies as fair use, you can file a counter-notice. However, proceed with caution and seek legal advice if necessary.

Appeal Process: YouTube has an appeal process for disputed takedown notices. If you file a counter-notice and the claimant does not respond within 14 business days, YouTube will restore your content. Be aware that filing a false counter-notice can have serious legal consequences.

Respecting Privacy

Respecting the privacy of individuals featured in your videos is crucial. Here are some tips to ensure you respect privacy rights:

Obtain Consent: If you're filming in a private location or featuring individuals prominently in your videos, obtain their consent. A simple release form can protect you from future disputes.

Blur Faces: When filming in public places, you may inadvertently capture people who do not wish to be on camera. Use video editing software to blur faces or other identifying features.

Avoid Personal Information: Be mindful of sharing personal information, both your own and others'. Avoid revealing addresses, phone numbers, or other sensitive details that could compromise privacy.

Handling Negative Feedback and Trolls

As your channel grows, you'll inevitably encounter negative feedback and trolls. Handling these situations professionally is key to maintaining a positive community.

Responding to Constructive Criticism: Not all negative feedback is bad. Constructive criticism can help you improve your content. Respond politely, thank the viewer for their feedback, and consider their suggestions.

Dealing with Trolls: Trolls are individuals who post inflammatory or off-topic comments to provoke others. Do not engage with trolls. Instead, use YouTube's moderation tools to hide or remove offensive comments and block repeat offenders.

Setting Community Guidelines: Establish clear community guidelines for your channel. Outline what is and isn't acceptable behavior in the comments section. Enforce these guidelines consistently to create a respectful environment.

Ethical Considerations in Content Creation

Beyond legal requirements, ethical considerations are important for building a reputable channel.

Avoid Clickbait: While catchy titles and thumbnails are important for attracting viewers, avoid misleading clickbait. Your content should deliver on the promises made in your title and thumbnail to maintain viewer trust.

Be Respectful: Create content that is respectful and considerate. Avoid offensive language, hate speech, and discriminatory remarks. Respect different opinions and foster a positive community.

Be Honest: Integrity is crucial for maintaining credibility. Be honest in your content, whether it's a product review, a tutorial, or a personal story. Your audience values authenticity and will appreciate your honesty.

Fact-Check: Ensure the information you provide is accurate. Misinformation can damage your reputation and mislead your audience. Take the time to research and verify facts before sharing them.

Takeaways

CHAPTER 8: LEGAL AND ETHICAL CONSIDERATIONS

Navigating the legal and ethical landscape of YouTube can seem daunting, but it's essential for building a successful and sustainable channel. Here's a quick recap of the key points:

Understand Copyright: Familiarize yourself with copyright laws and fair use. Use royalty-free content and seek permission when necessary.

Use Creative Commons: Utilize Creative Commons licenses to legally use other creators' work while respecting their terms.

Maintain Transparency: Disclose sponsored content, affiliate links, and product reviews to build trust with your audience and comply with legal requirements.

Handle Takedown Notices: Understand the DMCA process and respond appropriately to takedown notices.

Respect Privacy: Obtain consent, blur faces, and avoid sharing personal information to respect privacy rights.

Manage Feedback: Respond to constructive criticism, handle trolls professionally, and set clear community guidelines.

Uphold Ethics: Avoid clickbait, be respectful, honest, and fact-check your content to maintain credibility.

By adhering to these legal and ethical guidelines, you'll not only protect yourself from potential legal issues but also build a channel that viewers can trust and respect.

Chapter 9: Building a Personal Brand

You've established your YouTube channel, crafted engaging content, and started to build a loyal audience. Now it's time to take things to the next level by developing a strong personal brand. A personal brand isn't just about having a catchy logo or a memorable name; it's about creating a cohesive and authentic presence that resonates with your audience. Let's dive into the world of personal branding and explore how you can build a brand that stands out and connects with people on a deeper level.

Understanding Personal Branding

Personal branding is the process of defining and promoting what you stand for as an individual. It's about showcasing your personality, values, skills, and unique qualities in a way that makes you memorable and appealing to your audience. Your personal brand should reflect who you are, what you do, and why people should care.

Why is personal branding important? In a crowded digital landscape, your personal brand sets you apart from the competition. It helps you build trust and credibility, attract opportunities, and create a loyal following. A strong personal brand can turn viewers into fans and fans into advocates who actively support and promote your channel.

Defining Your Brand Identity

CHAPTER 9: BUILDING A PERSONAL BRAND

The first step in building your personal brand is defining your brand identity. This involves understanding who you are, what you offer, and how you want to be perceived. Here are some key elements to consider:

Your Values: What are the core principles that guide your actions and decisions? Your values should be reflected in your content and interactions with your audience. Whether it's authenticity, creativity, education, or entertainment, make sure your values are clear and consistent.

Your Personality: Your personality is what makes you unique and relatable. Are you funny, serious, adventurous, or thoughtful? Embrace your natural traits and let them shine through in your videos. Authenticity is key to building a genuine connection with your audience.

Your Skills and Expertise: What are you good at? What knowledge or skills do you bring to the table? Highlight your strengths and showcase your expertise in your niche. This establishes you as a credible source and builds trust with your viewers.

Your Unique Selling Proposition (USP): Your USP is what sets you apart from other creators in your niche. It's the unique angle or perspective that only you can offer. Identify what makes you different and use it to your advantage.

Creating a Visual Identity

Once you've defined your brand identity, it's time to create a visual identity that reflects it. Your visual identity includes your logo, color scheme, fonts, and overall aesthetic. These elements should be consistent across all your platforms to create a cohesive and recognizable brand.

Logo: Your logo is the visual representation of your brand. It should be simple, memorable, and reflective of your brand identity. Whether you design it yourself or hire a professional, make sure it's versatile and looks good in various sizes and formats.

Color Scheme: Choose a color palette that represents your brand's personality and values. Colors evoke emotions and can significantly impact how your brand is perceived. Stick to a consistent color scheme across your thumbnails, channel art, and social media to create a unified look.

Fonts: Select fonts that complement your brand's style. Use the same fonts consistently for your video titles, descriptions, and graphics. This helps create a professional and polished appearance.

Thumbnails and Channel Art: Your thumbnails and channel art are the first things viewers see when they visit your channel. Make sure they are visually appealing and convey the essence of your brand. Use high-quality images, bold text, and your brand's colors to make them stand out.

Crafting Your Brand Story

Your brand story is a powerful tool for connecting with your audience on an emotional level. It's the narrative that explains who you are, why you do what you do, and what you stand for. A compelling brand story can inspire and engage your viewers, making them more likely to become loyal fans.

Here's how to craft your brand story:

Start with Your Why: Why did you start your YouTube channel? What motivates you to create content? Your why is the foundation of your brand story. It's the passion and purpose that drive you and resonate with your audience.

Share Your Journey: Everyone loves a good story, especially one that includes challenges, triumphs, and personal growth. Share your journey with your audience, including the highs and lows. This makes you relatable and shows that you're human.

Highlight Your Values: Your values should be woven throughout your brand story. Show how they influence your decisions, content, and interactions. This helps your audience understand what you stand for and why they should support you.

Be Authentic: Authenticity is key to a compelling brand story. Don't try to be someone you're not. Be honest about your experiences, beliefs, and goals. Authenticity builds trust and fosters a deeper connection with your audience.

Communicating Your Brand

Building a personal brand isn't just about defining it; it's also about communicating it effectively. Every interaction you have with your audience, from your videos to your social media posts, should reinforce your brand identity.

Here are some tips for communicating your brand:

Consistent Messaging: Your messaging should be consistent across all platforms. Whether it's your video scripts, social media posts, or website copy, make sure your tone and style align with your brand identity.

Engage with Your Audience: Interact with your viewers in a way that reflects your brand's personality. Respond to comments, participate in discussions, and show appreciation for your audience's support. Engaging with your audience strengthens your brand and builds a loyal community.

Collaborate with Like-Minded Creators: Collaborations can help you reach a wider audience and reinforce your brand. Partner with creators who share your values and complement your content. This not only exposes you to new viewers but also enhances your credibility.

Leverage Social Media: Use social media to extend your brand beyond YouTube. Share behind-the-scenes content, updates, and personal insights that align with your brand identity. Social media is a great way to build a deeper connection with your audience and attract new followers.

Evolving Your Brand

Your personal brand is not static; it evolves as you grow and change. It's important to stay true to your core identity while being open to adaptation and improvement. Here's how to manage the evolution of your brand:

Stay Relevant: Keep up with trends and changes in your niche. Adapt your content and branding to stay relevant and appealing to your audience. However, make sure any changes align with your core values and identity.

Listen to Feedback: Pay attention to feedback from your audience. Use their insights to improve your content and brand. Being responsive to feedback shows that you value your audience and are committed to delivering the best experience.

Reevaluate Your Brand: Periodically review your brand identity and strategy. Are they still aligned with your goals and values? Are you effectively communicating your brand? Make adjustments as needed to ensure your brand remains strong and relevant.

Embrace Growth: As you grow as a creator, your brand will naturally evolve. Embrace this growth and use it to enhance your brand. Share your journey with your audience and let them be a part of your evolution.

Takeaways

Building a personal brand is essential for standing out in the crowded world of YouTube. It involves defining your brand identity, creating a visual identity, crafting a compelling brand story, and effectively communicating your brand to your audience.

Define Your Brand Identity: Understand your values, personality, skills, and unique selling proposition to create a strong brand foundation.

Create a Visual Identity: Develop a logo, color scheme, fonts, and overall aesthetic that reflect your brand and are consistent across all platforms.

Craft Your Brand Story: Share your why, your journey, and your values to connect with your audience on an emotional level.

Communicate Your Brand: Use consistent messaging, engage with your audience, collaborate with like-minded creators, and leverage social media to reinforce your brand.

Evolve Your Brand: Stay relevant, listen to feedback, reevaluate your brand periodically, and embrace growth as a creator.

By focusing on these elements, you can build a personal brand that resonates with your audience, sets you apart from the competition, and creates lasting connections with your viewers.

Chapter 10: Long-Term Growth and Sustainability

Congratulations! You've made it to the final chapter. By now, you've set up your channel, created high-quality content, started building an audience, and even monetized your efforts. But how do you ensure that your channel not only survives but thrives in the long run? Long-term growth and sustainability are about more than just keeping the lights on; it's about evolving, adapting, and maintaining your passion for creating content. Let's explore some strategies to help you sustain and grow your YouTube channel over the long haul.

Staying Motivated

Creating content consistently can be challenging, especially when you hit a creative slump or face burnout. Here are some tips to stay motivated and keep your creative juices flowing:

Set Realistic Goals: Break down your long-term vision into smaller, achievable goals. Celebrate small victories along the way to stay motivated. Whether it's reaching a certain number of subscribers or completing a series of videos, small milestones can keep you moving forward.

Take Breaks: It's important to give yourself time to recharge. Taking breaks can prevent burnout and keep you fresh. Use this time to explore new ideas,

CHAPTER 10: LONG-TERM GROWTH AND SUSTAINABILITY

relax, and come back with renewed energy and enthusiasm.

Find Inspiration: Stay inspired by consuming content from other creators, both within and outside your niche. Reading books, watching movies, or simply taking a walk can spark new ideas and keep your creativity alive.

Connect with Other Creators: Building relationships with other YouTubers can provide support, inspiration, and collaboration opportunities. Join creator communities, attend events, and engage with fellow creators to stay motivated and inspired.

Adapting to Change

The digital landscape is constantly evolving, and so should your channel. Here's how to stay adaptable and embrace change:

Stay Updated: Keep up with the latest trends, tools, and changes in the YouTube ecosystem. Follow industry news, participate in webinars, and join online communities to stay informed.

Be Open to Experimentation: Don't be afraid to try new things. Experiment with different content formats, styles, and topics to see what resonates with your audience. Adaptation often involves trial and error, so be willing to learn from your experiments.

Analyze Performance: Use YouTube Analytics to monitor your channel's performance and identify areas for improvement. Look for patterns and trends in your data to understand what's working and what's not. Use these insights to refine your content strategy.

Listen to Your Audience: Pay attention to feedback from your viewers. They can provide valuable insights into what they like and what they'd like to see more of. Engage with your audience through comments, polls, and social media to understand their preferences and adapt accordingly.

Diversifying Your Content

While consistency is key, diversifying your content can help you reach new audiences and keep your existing viewers engaged. Here are some ways to diversify your content:

Explore New Formats: Experiment with different video formats, such as tutorials, vlogs, interviews, and live streams. Variety keeps your content fresh and appealing to a broader audience.

Cover Different Topics: Expand your content by covering related topics within your niche. For example, if your channel is about fitness, you could also create videos on nutrition, mental health, and lifestyle.

Collaborate with Others: Partnering with other creators can bring new perspectives and ideas to your channel. Collaborations can also expose your channel to new audiences and provide fresh content for your viewers.

Create Series and Playlists: Develop content series or playlists around specific themes or topics. This encourages viewers to watch multiple videos and increases overall engagement and watch time.

Building a Strong Community

A strong, engaged community is the backbone of a sustainable YouTube channel. Here's how to foster a sense of community among your viewers:

Engage Regularly: Respond to comments, ask questions, and encourage discussions. Show appreciation for your viewers' support and make them feel valued.

CHAPTER 10: LONG-TERM GROWTH AND SUSTAINABILITY

Host Live Streams: Live streaming allows you to interact with your audience in real-time. Host Q&A sessions, tutorials, or casual hangouts to build a deeper connection with your viewers.

Create a Sense of Belonging: Use inclusive language and create content that makes your viewers feel like they're part of something special. Recognize and celebrate your community's milestones and achievements.

Offer Exclusive Content: Provide your most dedicated fans with exclusive content, such as behind-the-scenes footage, early access to videos, or members-only live streams. Platforms like Patreon or channel memberships can facilitate this.

Investing in Your Channel

Reinvesting some of your earnings back into your channel can help ensure long-term growth and sustainability. Here are some areas to consider investing in:

Better Equipment: Upgrading your camera, microphone, lighting, and editing software can significantly improve the quality of your videos. High-quality content attracts more viewers and keeps them engaged.

Outsourcing Tasks: As your channel grows, you might find it challenging to handle everything yourself. Consider outsourcing tasks like video editing, graphic design, and social media management to professionals. This allows you to focus on creating content while maintaining high production standards.

Marketing and Promotion: Invest in marketing your channel through paid promotions, collaborations, or hiring a marketing expert. Effective marketing can help you reach a larger audience and grow your channel faster.

Education and Training: Continuously improve your skills by taking courses, attending workshops, and learning from industry experts. Investing in your education can help you stay ahead of the curve and produce better content.

Monetization Strategies

To ensure long-term sustainability, it's important to diversify your revenue streams. Here are some monetization strategies to consider:

Ad Revenue: Continue to optimize your videos for ad revenue through the YouTube Partner Program. Create longer videos, place ads strategically, and engage your audience to maximize earnings.

Sponsorships: Partner with brands for sponsored content. Reach out to companies that align with your niche and offer value to your audience. Negotiate fair terms and maintain transparency with your viewers.

Affiliate Marketing: Promote products or services through affiliate links. Earn commissions from sales generated through your links. Ensure the products you promote are relevant and valuable to your audience.

Merchandise: Sell branded merchandise such as t-shirts, mugs, and stickers. Use platforms like Teespring or Merchbar to design, produce, and sell your merch directly through your channel.

Crowdfunding: Platforms like Patreon and Ko-fi allow your fans to support you financially. Offer exclusive content and perks to your patrons in exchange for their support.

Digital Products: Create and sell digital products such as e-books, online courses, and exclusive video content. Use platforms like Gumroad or your own website to distribute your products.

Maintaining Work-Life Balance

CHAPTER 10: LONG-TERM GROWTH AND SUSTAINABILITY

Sustaining a successful YouTube channel requires hard work, but it's also important to maintain a healthy work-life balance. Here are some tips to achieve this:

Set Boundaries: Establish clear boundaries between your work and personal life. Set specific work hours and stick to them. Avoid working late into the night or during family time.

Prioritize Self-Care: Take care of your physical and mental health. Exercise regularly, eat healthily, get enough sleep, and make time for hobbies and relaxation.

Delegate Tasks: As your channel grows, delegate tasks to others. Hire help or collaborate with team members to share the workload. This allows you to focus on what you do best and reduces stress.

Take Breaks: Schedule regular breaks to recharge and prevent burnout. Use this time to disconnect from work and engage in activities that rejuvenate you.

Reflect and Reassess: Periodically reflect on your goals, priorities, and workload. Reassess your approach and make adjustments as needed to maintain a healthy balance.

Takeaways

Ensuring long-term growth and sustainability for your YouTube channel involves staying motivated, adapting to change, diversifying your content, building a strong community, investing in your channel, and maintaining a healthy work-life balance.

Stay Motivated: Set realistic goals, take breaks, find inspiration, and connect with other creators to stay motivated.

Adapt to Change: Stay updated with industry trends, be open to experimentation, analyze performance, and listen to your audience.

Diversify Your Content: Explore new formats, cover different topics, collaborate with others, and create series and playlists.

Build a Strong Community: Engage regularly, host live streams, create a sense of belonging, and offer exclusive content.

Invest in Your Channel: Upgrade equipment, outsource tasks, invest in marketing, and continue your education.

Diversify Revenue Streams: Optimize ad revenue, seek sponsorships, engage in affiliate marketing, sell merchandise, offer digital products, and use crowdfunding platforms.

Maintain Work-Life Balance: Set boundaries, prioritize self-care, delegate tasks, take breaks, and reflect and reassess regularly.

By implementing these strategies, you can build a sustainable and successful YouTube channel that continues to grow and thrive over the long term.

Conclusion: Your YouTube Journey Awaits

Congratulations! You've made it through the YouTube Starter Kit, and now you're equipped with the knowledge and tools to embark on your YouTube journey. Creating a successful YouTube channel is no small feat, but you've shown the dedication and enthusiasm needed to get started. Let's take a moment to reflect on what we've covered and look ahead to the exciting road before you.

Reflecting on the Journey

Starting your own YouTube channel is like setting out on an adventure. It begins with a single idea, a spark of creativity that ignites the desire to share your passion with the world. Remember when you first brainstormed your niche? Whether it was fitness, cooking, gaming, or something entirely unique, it all started with identifying what you love. This passion is the cornerstone of your channel and will keep you motivated even when the going gets tough.

Next came planning and setting up your channel. You navigated through the technical setup, designed a visually appealing channel, and crafted a compelling description. These foundational steps are crucial for making a great first impression and attracting your initial audience.

As you moved forward, creating high-quality content became your focus. You learned about the importance of scripting, filming techniques, and editing skills. Producing engaging videos that captivate your audience is the heart of your YouTube channel. Each video is a piece of you, a glimpse into your world, and a chance to connect with others who share your interests.

Growing your audience and monetizing your channel were the next big milestones. You discovered strategies to promote your content, engage with your community, and diversify your revenue streams. Building a loyal audience and turning your passion into a sustainable income source are significant achievements that require continuous effort and creativity.

Legal and ethical considerations reminded you of the importance of respecting copyright laws, maintaining transparency, and upholding ethical standards. Navigating these aspects responsibly builds trust with your audience and ensures a long-lasting and positive reputation.

Finally, we discussed the importance of building a personal brand, staying adaptable, and ensuring long-term growth and sustainability. These elements help you stand out in a crowded digital landscape and keep your content fresh and relevant.

Looking Ahead

Now that you're equipped with all this knowledge, what's next? The journey doesn't end here—it's just beginning. Here are some final tips to help you continue your YouTube adventure with confidence and enthusiasm:

Stay Curious and Keep Learning: The digital world is ever-evolving, and there's always something new to learn. Stay curious and open to new ideas, techniques, and trends. Attend workshops, read articles, watch tutorials, and never stop improving your skills.

Be Consistent but Flexible: Consistency is key to building and maintaining an audience, but don't be afraid to pivot if something isn't working. Adapt to feedback, experiment with new formats, and keep refining your approach. Flexibility allows you to grow and evolve with your audience's needs and interests.

Balance Passion and Practicality: While passion drives creativity, practicality ensures sustainability. Set realistic goals, manage your time effectively, and maintain a healthy work-life balance. Remember, it's a marathon, not a sprint.

Celebrate Milestones: Take time to celebrate your achievements, no matter how small. Each milestone, whether it's gaining your first 100 subscribers or completing a challenging video project, is a step forward. Celebrating these moments keeps you motivated and reminds you of how far you've come.

Build Relationships: Networking with other creators and engaging with your audience are invaluable. Collaboration and community support can lead to new opportunities and help you grow. Be genuine in your interactions and build relationships based on mutual respect and shared interests.

Stay True to Yourself: Authenticity is your greatest asset. Stay true to your voice, values, and vision. Your audience is drawn to you because of who you are, so let your personality shine through in everything you do.

Challenges and Rewards

Let's be honest: running a YouTube channel isn't always a smooth ride. You'll face challenges, from technical glitches to creative blocks and fluctuating viewer engagement. However, these hurdles are part of the journey and offer valuable learning experiences. Embrace them with a positive attitude and use them as opportunities to grow and improve.

The rewards, both tangible and intangible, make the effort worthwhile. There's nothing quite like the satisfaction of seeing your hard work pay off—whether it's through a growing subscriber count, positive comments from viewers, or even the thrill of earning your first paycheck from YouTube. Beyond these rewards, there's the fulfillment that comes from creating content that resonates with people and building a community around your passion.

Inspiring Others

One of the most rewarding aspects of being a YouTuber is the ability to inspire others. Your content has the power to educate, entertain, and motivate your viewers. You might be teaching someone a new skill, providing a moment of laughter in a tough day, or encouraging someone to pursue their own passion. Recognize the impact you can have and strive to create content that makes a positive difference in your viewers' lives.

Future Growth

As you look to the future, think about how you want your channel to grow. What are your long-term goals? Perhaps you want to expand into new content areas, launch a merchandise line, or even turn your YouTube channel into a full-time career. Whatever your aspirations, keep them in mind as you continue to create and connect with your audience.

Consider the potential for branching out beyond YouTube. Your personal brand can extend to other platforms, such as a blog, podcast, or social media channels. Diversifying your presence can help you reach new audiences and build a more robust and resilient brand.

The Road Ahead

Your journey as a YouTuber is unique and filled with endless possibilities. Embrace the adventure with enthusiasm, resilience, and a sense of humor. There will be ups and downs, but each step forward brings you closer to your goals. Remember why you started, stay true to your passion, and keep creating

CONCLUSION: YOUR YOUTUBE JOURNEY AWAITS

content that you love and believe in.

As you continue on this path, keep an open mind and a willingness to learn and adapt. The landscape of digital content creation is dynamic, and staying ahead of the curve requires both creativity and strategy. With the right mindset and dedication, there's no limit to what you can achieve.

Final Thoughts

You're now ready to embark on your YouTube journey with confidence and excitement. You have the tools, knowledge, and passion needed to create a successful and sustainable channel. Embrace the challenges, celebrate the victories, and always strive to make a positive impact through your content.

The world is waiting to see what you'll create next. Your unique voice, perspective, and creativity have the power to inspire and connect with others in meaningful ways. So, go ahead and hit that record button—your YouTube journey awaits!

Made in the USA
Las Vegas, NV
22 November 2024

12401745R00046